Scientists
USE TOOLS

BY ANNETTE GULATI

rourkeeducationalmedia.com

Before & After Reading Activities

Teaching Focus:

Concepts of Print- Have students find capital letters and punctuation in a sentence. Ask students to explain the purpose for using them in a sentence.

Before Reading:

Building Academic Vocabulary and Background Knowledge

Before reading a book, it is important to set the stage for your child or student by using pre-reading strategies. This will help them develop their vocabulary, increase their reading comprehension, and make connections across the curriculum.

1. *Read the title and look at the cover. Let's make predictions about what this book will be about.*
2. *Take a picture walk by talking about the pictures/photographs in the book. Implant the vocabulary as you take the picture walk. Be sure to talk about the text features such as headings, Table of Contents, glossary, bolded words, captions, charts/ diagrams, or Index.*
3. *Have students read the first page of text with you then have students read the remaining text.*
4. *Strategy Talk – use to assist students while reading.*
    - Get your mouth ready
    - Look at the picture
    - Think…does it make sense
    - Think…does it look right
    - Think…does it sound right
    - Chunk it – by looking for a part you know
5. *Read it again.*

Content Area Vocabulary

Use glossary words in a sentence.

compares

mass

measurements

observations

temperature

volume

After Reading:

Comprehension and Extension Activity

After reading the book, work on the following questions with your child or students in order to check their level of reading comprehension and content mastery.

1. *Name some tools scientists use in their jobs.* (Summarize)
2. *How does a scientist measure the temperature of liquid?* (Asking Questions)
3. *Why would a scientist need a microscope?* (Asking Questions)
4. *Have you ever used a scientific tool? What was it? What did you use it for?* (Text to Self Connection)

Extension Activity: Be a Scientist!

Go on a hunt around your home. How many tools can you find? How are they alike? How are they different? Are some used for measuring? How do the tools make your life easier?

Table of Contents

ROurke
Educational Media
rourkeeducationalmedia.com

Study

Scientists use tools to study the world.

They use tools to stay safe.
Safety goggles protect their eyes.
Gloves guard their hands.

Scientists often work with dangerous liquids.

Observe

Scientists use tools to make **observations**.

Microscopes make small objects appear bigger.

Measure

They use tools to take **measurements.**
A ruler measures length.

Length is measured in inches or centimeters (cm).

A stopwatch measures time.

Time is measured in seconds, minutes, and hours.

A measuring cup measures the **volume** of a liquid.

Scientists measure volume in milliliters (mL) or liters (L).

A thermometer shows the liquid's **temperature.**

Scientists measure temperature using the Fahrenheit scale (°F) or the Celsius scale (°C).

Scientists use scales or balances to find the **mass** of an object.

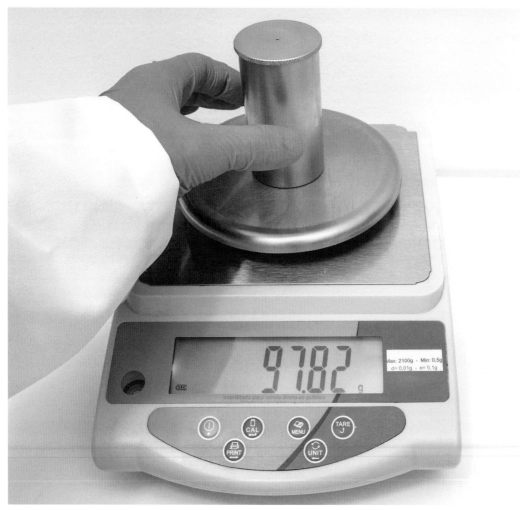

Scientists measure mass in grams (g) or kilograms (kg).

A balance **compares** two objects and tells the scientist which one is heavier.

Record

Scientists record everything they study. They use cameras.

Cameras help scientists remember how something looks.

They write in notebooks. They record and study their data using computers.

Scientists compare data using charts and graphs.

Scientists work in the lab or in the field. Tools make their jobs safer and easier.

Scientists often work together and share ideas.

Make Your Own Balance

You will need:

- ✓ a hanger with notches

- ✓ string

- ✓ two plastic buckets with handles

- ✓ objects to measure *(bark, flowers, grass, rocks, stones)*

Directions:

1. Hang the hanger on a knob or rod. Make sure it has room to swing.
2. Cut two equal pieces of string. Tie one to the handle of each bucket.
3. Tie one bucket to each end of the hanger.
4. Put one object in each bucket. Which is heavier? Try again with other objects.

Photo Glossary

compares (kuhm-PAIRS): Observes two or more things and thinks about how they're the same or different.

mass (mas): The amount of physical matter that an object contains.

measurements (MEZH-ur-muhnts): Amounts figured out by measuring.

observations (uhb-zur-VAY-shuhns): Information noticed when looking and listening very closely.

temperature (TEM-pur-uh-chur): A measure of how cold or hot something is.

volume (VAHL-yoom): The amount of space taken up by an object or a liquid in a container.

Index

Further Reading

Howell, Sara, *Chemists at Work*, Rosen Publishing, 2018.

Mould, Steve, *How to Be a Scientist,* DK Publishing, 2017.

Franco, Mishou, *I Can Be a Scientist,* Gareth Stevens Publishing, 2017.

Meet The Author!
www.meetREMauthors.com

About the Author

Annette Gulati loves exploring the world and learning new things. She always uses her favorite tools—a camera, a pen, and a notebook—to record everything she learns. She lives in Seattle, Washington with her family.

www.rourkeeducationalmedia.com

PHOTO CREDITS: Cover ©teekid, Title Page ©RobinOlimb , Table of Contents ©teekid, Page 5 ©shironosov, Page 7 ©DragonImages, Page 9 and 23 ©fotostorm, Page 10 ©DNY59, Page 11 and 22 ©Mny-Jhee, Page 12 and 23 ©studiocasper, Page 13 and 23 ©studiocasper, Page 14 and 22 ©Thiago Santos, Page 15 and 22 ©quan long, Page 16 ©stevanovicigor, Page 17 ©shironosov, Page 18 ©sanjeri,

Edited by: Keli Sipperley
Cover and Interior design by: Kathy Walsh

Library of Congress PCN Data
Scientists Use Tools / Annette Gulati
(Starting with STEAM)
ISBN 978-1-64156-426-7 (hard cover)(alk. paper)
ISBN 978-1-64156-552-3 (soft cover)
ISBN 978-1-64156-674-2 (e-Book)
Library of Congress Control Number: 2018930447
Printed in the United States of America, North Mankato, Minnesota

24